The Howling Pandemonium and other noisy poems

031290

The Howling Pandemonium and other noisy poems

Compiled by Zenka and Ian Woodward
Illustrated by Julie Park

Blackie

For
Edge Grove School
and
St Nicholas House School

Copyright © 1990 Zenka and Ian Woodward
in this collection
Illustrations © 1990 Julie Park
First published 1990 by Blackie and Son Ltd

All rights reserved. No part of this publication may be reproduced, stored in a retrieval system, or transmitted in any form or by any means, electronic, mechanical, photocopying, recording or otherwise without the written permission of the Publishers.

British Library Cataloguing in Publication Data
The Howling pandemonium.
1. Children's poetry in English—Anthologies
I. Woodward, Ian II. Woodward, Zenka
821.00809282

ISBN 0-216-92738-2

Blackie and Son Ltd
7 Leicester Place
London WC2H 7BP

About the Editors

Zenka and Ian Woodward have compiled numerous poetry anthologies for young readers. Their collections include *Poems for Fun, Comic and Curious Verse* and *Spine Tinglers*. Their previous anthology for Blackie, *There Are Monsters About*, was selected for the *Children's Book of the Year Catalogue 1987*. The Woodwards have homes in Hertfordshire and a Spanish fishing village, where they live with their two children, Philip and Stefanie.

Introduction

Funny thing, noise

> And then there crept
> A little noiseless noise among the leaves,
> Born of the very sigh that silence heaves.

When John Keats wrote these lines at the beginning of the last century — they appear in his lovely poem 'I Stood Tiptoe' — noise was something quite different to the sort of noise we hear around us today. Noise was sad and sweet and even mad, according to Emily Dickinson in her poem on page 12 ('The Saddest Noise'). Noise was a very natural thing to the early poets. William Blake saw green woods laughing 'with the voice of joy' (page 42, 'Laughing Song') and, to Christina Rossetti, the wind had 'such a rainy sound' ('Storm-wind', page 43).

This was long before the age of *big* noise . . . before pop music roared from transistor radios, before jet aircraft roared overhead and before loudspeakers blew out your ear-drums at parties. Some of these 'modern' noises run merrily through these pages: speedway racing and thundering express trains.

But not all noise is noisy and we have tried to include a few of these gentler sounds. The delicate 'Humming-Bird' on page 14 is one of our favourites. It is quite different, of course, to the crashing, bashing, tooting, hooting that is going on in the poem by Eleanor Farjeon (page 17) from which this book takes its name.

We have enjoyed tracking down these poems. Some are funny. Some are thoughtful. Some, downright noisy. But all, we think, have an element of surprise about them. We hope you think so, too.

ZENKA and IAN WOODWARD

Another Day

Boys shout,
Girls giggle,
Pencils write,
Squiggle squiggle.
Get it wrong,
Cross it out,
Bell's gone!
All out!

Balls bounce,
Hands clap,
Skipping ropes,
Slap slap.
Hand-stands,
By the wall,
Sara Williams
Best of all.
Boys fight,
Girls flee,
Teacher's gone
And spilt
His tea!
Clatter bang!
Big din!
Whistle goes,
All in!

All quiet,
No sound,
Hear worms,
Under ground.
Chalk squeaks,
Clock creeps,
Head on desk,
Boy sleeps.

Home time!
Glory be!
Mum's got
Chips for tea.
Warm fire,
Full belly,
Sit down,
Watch telly.

Bed time,
Creep away,
Dream until,
Another day.

JOHN CUNLIFFE

The Wheel Around the World

If all the world's children
wanted to play holding hands
they could happily make
a wheel around the sea.

If all the world's children
wanted to play holding hands
they could be sailors
and build a bridge across the seas.

What a beautiful chorus we would make
singing around the earth
if all the humans in the world
wanted to dance holding hands!

ANON

The Saddest Noise, the Sweetest Noise

The saddest noise, the sweetest noise,
The maddest noise that grows,
The birds, they make it in the spring,
At night's delicious close

Between the March and April line,
That magical frontier
Beyond which summer hesitates,
Almost too heavenly near.

EMILY DICKINSON

Hearing the Cry of the Cock

You're only an ordinary animal,
But every morning
Your cry brings in the day.
Cry of the cock!
You wake the people from sleep.
There's no doubt about it —
Your work is important!

HO CHI MINH

Humming-Bird

Humming-bird, humming-bird, why don't you
   hum?
I do not hum because I am dumb.
Then why are you called humming-bird of all
   things?
Because of the noise that I make with my wings.

ODETTE THOMAS

Noise

Billy is blowing his trumpet,
Bertie is banging a tin;
Betty is crying for mummy
And Bob has pricked Ben with a pin.
Baby is crying out loudly;
He's out on the lawn in his pram.
I am the only silent one
And I've eaten all of the jam.

JAMES PARKER

Music Makers

My auntie plays the piccolo,
My uncle plays the flute,
They practise every night at ten,
Tweetly tweet *Toot-toot!*

My granny plays the banjo,
My grandad plays the drum,
They practise every night at nine,
Plankety plank *Bumm-bumm!!*

My sister plays the tuba,
My brother plays guitar,
They practise every night at six,
Twankity *Ooom-pa-pa!!!*

My mother plays the mouth organ,
My daddy plays oboe,
They practise every night at eight,
Pompity-pom suck-blow!!!!

GRACE EBON

The Howling Pandemonium

Crash and
    CLANG!
Bash and
    BANG!
And up in the road the Jazz-Man sprang!
The One-Man-Jazz-Band playing in the street,
Drums with his Elbows, Cymbals with his Feet,
Pipes with his Mouth, Accordian with his Hand,
Playing all his Instruments to Beat the Band!
  TOOT and
    Tingle!
  HOOT and
    Jingle!
Oh, what a Clatter! how the tunes all mingle!
Twenty children couldn't make as much Noise *as*
The Howling Pandemonium of the One-Man-Jazz!

ELEANOR FARJEON

I'm a Treble in the Choir

In the Choir I'm a treble
And my singing is the debbel!
I'm a treble in the Choir!
They sing high but I sing higher.
Treble singing's VERY high,
But the highest high am I!
Soon I'll burst like any bubble:
I'm a treble — that's the trouble!

EDMOND KAPP

No Wonder I Can't Get to Sleep

I can hear the trees whispering
    the cats purring
    the dogs barking
No wonder I can't get to sleep.

I can hear my dad in a rage
tearing up a page into little bits
while my mother sits crying
No wonder I can't get to sleep.

MARSHA PROVIDENCE

Milk

Every morning at six o'clock
Ma Dookie brings the milk
She comes in front and shouts 'Oo-Oo'
And then she cries 'Mil-lik'.

ODETTE THOMAS

Snores

'There's the cheeky snore, an' the squeaky snore,
 and the snore that sounds like silk;
There's the creamy, dreamy kind of snore that
 comes of drinkin' milk;
There's the raspy snore, an' the gaspy snore, an'
 the snore that's 'ard to wake.
An' the snore that's 'arf a jackass larf an' the hiss
 of a startled snake.
There's the snore that shows its owner's shick, an'
 the one that shows 'e's not,
And one 'oose owner I'd like to kick, the worst of
 all the lot.
It's a kind of cross between a calf an' a pig that's
 dyin' 'ard
With a bit thrown in from the mornin' din out in
 the poultry yard.

'There's also the snore that softly sighs like the
   close of an evenin' hymn,
As if a bloke 'ad just got wise 'e'd lorst an 'arf a
   jim.
I've 'eard 'em snore in concert pitch an' also a
   trifle flat,
With snores that orfen drop a stitch, then bustle
   an' get the bat.
There's the snore that trickles the keyhole track
   like onions bein' fried,
And the snore of the bachelor on 'ees back an' the
   spinster on 'er side.
There's the haughty snore an' the snorty snore of
   blokes wots prim an' proud,
An' the snore of the cove wot owes a score, 'oose
   conscience 'as 'im cowed!

E G MURPHY

My Noisy Brother

My noisy brother's always noisy,
Going to bed, watching TV,
Waking up in the morning, always noisy.

My noisy brother is noisy at dinner,
He shouts GOODBYE loudly when going to
    secondary school
He shouts like an elephant for fish and chips.

At night when my brother goes to sleep
He snores like my 40-year-old dad,
And when he wakes up in the morning
He yells like mad for his breakfast,
But he's just my noisy brother.

My brother Muntaquim is not noisy at school,
But when he comes home the bombardment starts
Like a stool throwing.
He's the noisiest brother I ever had,
But he's still my noisy brother.

KASHIM CHOWDHURY

When I Am Angry

When I get angry I start
    screaming
and screeching
    raging
and hating
    smashing
and biting
    crying
and punching
    leaving
and breaking
    throwing
and destroying
    steamed up
and blowing up
    slam doors
and stamping
    exploding
and strangling
    cuddling
and kissing
    sorrys
and quiet again.

IAN WHITE

Last Word

Dad says:
Stop doing that.
So the boy stuck his tongue out.
Dad says:
Don't stick your tongue out at me.
So the boy says:
I'm not. I'm just licking my lips.

Later:
BANG BANG BANG BANG
Dad says:
Stop jumping up and down up there
I can't stand the noise.
And the girl says:
I'm not jumping. I'm hopping.
Dad says:

Some people always get the last word.

MICHAEL ROSEN

Wow! Wow! Wow!

(To be recited by one person, with two or more friends making the sounds of the Chorus.)

Speak roughly to your little boy,
    And beat him when he sneezes:
He only does it to annoy,
    Because he knows it teases.

Chorus

WOW! WOW! WOW!

I speak severely to my boy,
    I beat him when he sneezes;
For he can thoroughly enjoy
    The pepper when he pleases!

Chorus

WOW! WOW! WOW!

LEWIS CARROLL

The Mutinous Jack-in-a-box

Why should I always jump
when they press that stupid button?
Always at their call?
Next time . . . *next* time . . .
I'll stick my tongue out at them.
I'll spit!
I'll shout rude words!
I'll pull horrid faces!
I'll make their baby cry
and turn their milk sour.
I will!
Just you wait and see!
They can't fool me;
not forever a slave;
next time I'll be brave.

BOOOOOOOOIIIINNNNNNNGGGG
 GGGGGGGGG
 !!!!!

Oh dear, I did it again,
Up I jumped,
Grinning as though I had no brain;
But . . . just you wait and see.
Next time I'll do it;
I will . . . I will . . .

JOHN CUNLIFFE

The Recruiting Sergeant

Come here to me, my merry, merry men,
    Said a sergeant at the fair;
And the bumpkins all were very merry men,
    And they all came running there.
Fat and spare, round and square,
    See them stare with noddles bare.
And the piper piped an air,
    And the drummer drummed his share,
With a rub-a-dub, rub-a-dub, row dow dow,
And the little dogs answered bow, wow, wow,
   And the boys cried out Hurrah!
    Hurrah! Hurrah! Hurrah!

PHILIP KATZ

O What is That Sound?

O what is that sound which so thrills the ear
   Down in the valley drumming, drumming?
Only the scarlet soldiers, dear,
   The soldiers coming.

W H AUDEN

Jeremiah Obadiah

Jeremiah Obadiah, puff, puff, puff.
When he gives his messages he snuffs, snuffs, snuffs,
When he goes to school by day, he roars, roars, roars,
When he goes to bed at night he snores, snores, snores,
When he goes to Christmas treats he eats plum-duff,
Jeremiah Obadiah, puff, puff, puff.

ANON

Noisy Little Puffer Train

Puffer train, Puffer train,
Noisy little Puffer train.
If you're going to the sea,
Puffer train, Oh please take me.
Ff-Ff-Ff, Sh-Sh-Sh
Ch-Ch-Ch-Ch-Ch, Ch-Ch-Ch,
Noisy little Puffer train.

ANON

Railway Line

Dumps beside the railway track —
   Gold with flowers,
   Red with flame;
Feathered grasses on the black
Of no-man's land with no-man's name.

Up . . . train . . . comes . . .
   Tumbril-Tumbril,
   Stick-at-a-wicket-a-rack.
   Rick-at-a-rack
   Flick-at-a-wicket-a-rack.
Passss. . . . Passss . . . . Passss
   Guard's . . . van . . . gone . . .

Embankments on the railway lines —
   Patched with lupins,
   Sunk in weed;
Iron fences chained by vines,
Allotments, tangled, gone to seed.

Up . . . train . . . comes . . .
  Tumbril-Tumbril,
  Stick-at-a-wicket-a-rack.
  Rick-at-a-rack.
  Flick-at-a-wicket-a-rack.
  . . . lick-at-a-wick.
  . . . . ick-at-a . . . . . ick-at-a . . . . .
  Passssssssssssss . . . .
  Train's . . . . gone . . .

MARIAN LINES

Speedway Racing

They line up together,
These monsters of speed,
Then, quicker than lightning,
There's some in the lead.
They come to a corner
Most dreaded of all,
Too closely they take it
And three of them fall.
But on go the rest
With a rush and a roar,
Faster and faster
Than ever before;
The favourite foremost,
His rival behind,
They take the last turning,
Up-curving and blind.
The leader leaps forward,
And then the flag drops,
He cuts off his engine,
And soon as he stops,
And lifts up his helmet,
Then loud in his ears
Rings thunder of clapping,
And cheers upon cheers.

ANA BALDUQUE

Aeroplanes, Aeroplanes All in a Row

Aeroplanes, aeroplanes all in a row;
Aeroplanes, aeroplanes ready to go.
Hark, they're beginning to buzz and to hum,
Bzzzzz;
Engines all working so come along, come.
Now we are flying up into the sky,
Faster and faster, oh, ever so high.

ANON

Speedboats

Speedboats, bright blue, yellow and red,
Shooting all morning across the bay,
Riding the waves of the deep waterway,
Like birds in storm you drive ahead.

Speedboats, I can see you now from the cliff,
Parting the breakers with mighty power,
Racing at one hundred miles an hour,
You leave behind every yacht and skiff.

Speedboats, I can hear your strong engines whine,
Filling the air with a sudden roar,
Deafening the people there on the shore,
How I wish that one of you were mine.

LEONARD CLARK

Death of the Steel Works

Thud, bang, clash, roar,
Thud, bang, clash, roar,
Rollers humming,
Trucks chugging,
Bright lights flashing,
Hot steel hissing,
Thud, bang, clash, roar.

Tap, tap, whizz,
Tap, tap, whizz,
Taps in the office,
Hissing in the towers,
The roar of water,
The bubble of iron,
Tap, tap, whizz.

Tumble, tumble, roar,
Tumble, tumble, roar,
Coal-tipping trucks,
Empty their loads in a rush,
Intensive heat hoards the furnace,
Red hot coke burns up to the surface,
Tumber, tumble, roar.

Alas, these sounds are heard no more,
No footsteps leaving the mill,
CLOSED is the sign upon the door,
Now all is quiet and still.

CAROLINE LAMB

Chipper, Chopper Joe

Chip-chop, chip-chop, Chipper, Chopper Joe,
Chip-chop, chip-chop, Chipper, Chopper Joe.
One big blow!
Ouch! my toe!
Chipper Chopper Joe chops wood just so!

ARTHUR CLASON

All Day I Hear The Noise of Waters

All day I hear the noise of waters
   Making moan,
Sad as the sea-bird is, when going
   Forth alone,
He hears the winds cry to the waters'
   Monotone.
The grey winds, the cold winds are blowing
   Where I go.
I hear the noise of many waters
   Far below.
All day, all night, I hear them flowing
   To and fro.

JAMES JOYCE

Down in Yonder Meadow

Down in yonder meadow where the green grass
   grows,
Pretty Pollie Pillicote bleaches her clothes.
She sang, she sang, she sang, oh, so sweet,
She sang, *Oh, come over!* across the street.
He kissed her, he kissed her, he bought her a
   gown,
A gown of rich cramasie out of the town.
He bought her a gown and a guinea gold ring,
A guinea, a guinea, a guinea gold ring;
Up street, and down, shine the windows made of
   glass,
Oh, isn't Pollie Pillicote a braw young lass?
Cherries in her cheeks, and ringlets her hair,
Hear her singing *Handy, Dandy* up and down the
   stair.

ANON

Laughing Song

When the green woods laugh with the voice of
   joy,
And the dimpling stream runs laughing by;
When the air does laugh with our merry wit,
And the green hill laughs with the noise of it;

When the meadows laugh with lively green,
And the grasshopper laughs in the merry scene;
When Mary and Susan and Emily
With their sweet round mouths sing 'Ha, ha, he!'

When the painted birds laugh in the shade,
When our table with cherries and nuts is spread:
Come live, and be merry, and join with me
To sing the sweet chorus of 'Ha, ha, he!'

WILLIAM BLAKE

Storm-wind

The wind has such a rainy sound
  Moaning through the town,
The sea has such a windy sound —
  Will the ships go down?

The apples in the orchard
  Tumble from their tree —
Oh will the ships go down, go down,
  In the windy sea?

CHRISTINA ROSSETTI

The Wind Was on the Withered Heath

The wind was on the withered heath,
but in the forest stirred no leaf:
there shadows lay by night and day,
and dark things silent crept beneath.

The wind came down from mountains cold,
and like a tide it roared and rolled;
the branches groaned, the forest moaned,
and leaves were laid upon the mould.

The wind went on from West to East;
all movement in the forest ceased,
but shrill and harsh across the marsh
its whistling voices were released.

The grasses hissed, their tassels bent,
the reeds were rattling — on it went.
o'er shaken pool under heavens cool
where racing clouds were torn and rent.

It passed the lonely Mountain bare
and swept above the dragon's lair:
there black and dark lay boulders stark
and flying smoke was in the air.

It left the world and took its flight
over the wide seas of the night
The moon set sail upon the gale,
and stars were fanned to leaping light.

J R R TOLKIEN

Windy Nights

Whenever the moon and stars are set,
   Whenever the wind is high,
All night long in the dark and wet,
   A man goes riding by.
Late in the night when the fires are out,
Why does he gallop and gallop about?

Whenever the trees are crying aloud,
   And ships are tossed at sea,
By, on the highway, low and loud,
   By at the gallop goes he.
By at the gallop he goes, and then
By he comes back at the gallop again.

ROBERT LOUIS STEVENSON

Thunderstorm

Rain is falling
down,
down,
it sparkles
flashes
pouring
splashing
diamonds on the window pane

Lightning flashing
It shines up my bedroom
And it streams through the air

Thunder crashes
Roaring
Banging
Noisy
Smashing
Thumping
Drums beating

DANIELLE BROWN

Noises in the Night

Midnight's bell goes ting, ting, ting, ting, ting,
Then dogs do howl, and not a bird does sing
But the nightingale, and she goes twit, twit, twit.
Owls then on every bough do sit,
Ravens croak on chimney tops,
The cricket in the chamber hops,
And the cats cry mew, mew, mew.
The nibbling mouse is not asleep,
But he goes peep, peep, peep, peep, peep,
And the cats cry mew, mew, mew,
   And still the cats cry mew, mew, mew.

THOMAS MIDDLETON

Bell-song

In the greenwood stands a chapel
Underneath an apple-tree,
In the greenwood stands a chapel
Underneath a yellow apple.
Ding-dong! ding-dong! ding-dong! ding-dong!
Ding-dong! ding-a-ding-a-dong!

No one goes inside the chapel
Underneath the apple-tree;
No one goes inside the chapel,
No one comes to shake an apple.
Ding-dong! ding-dong! ding-dong! ding-dong!
Ding-dong! ding-a-ding-a-dong!

But like bells above the chapel
Shakes the yellow apple-tree;
Like sweet bells above the chapel
Shakes the yellow, mellow apple.
Ding-dong! ding-dong! ding-dong! ding-dong!
Ding-dong! ding-a-ding-a-dong!

ELEANOR FARJEON

Bishopsgate

Bishopsgate Without!
Bishopsgate Within!
What a clamour at the Gate,
O what a din!
Inside and Outside
The Bishops bang and shout,
Outside crying, 'Let me In!'
Inside, 'Let me Out!'

ELEANOR FARJEON

On the Ning Nang Nong

On the Ning Nang Nong
Where the Cows go Bong!
And the Monkeys all say Boo!
There's a Nong Nang Ning
Where the trees go Ping!
And the tea pots Jibber Jabber Joo.
On the Nong Ning Nang
All the mice go Clang!
And you just can't catch 'em when they do!
So it's Ning Nang Nong!
Cows go Bong!
Nong Nang Ning!
Trees go Ping!
Nong Ning Nang!
The mice go Clang!
What a *noisy* place to belong,
Is the Ning Nang Ning Nang Nong!

SPIKE MILLIGAN

Eletelephony

Once there was an elephant,
Who tried to use the telephant —
No No! I mean an elephone
Who tried to use the telephone —
(Dear me! I am not certain quite
That even now I've got it right.)

Howe'er it was, he got his trunk
Entangled in the telephunk;
The more he tried to get it free,
The louder buzzed the telephee —
(I fear I'd better drop the song
Of elephop and telephong!)

LAURA E RICHARDS

The Panther Roars

The panther roars on the mountain,
The tiger roars in the forest,
The king roars on his throne
With sword and shield in hand.

ANON

The Air Was Filled with a Clamour Appalling

The air was filled with a clamour appalling
Of howling, yowling and caterwauling,
Mewing, mooing,
Chirping, cooing.
Cackling, cock-a-doodle-doing,
Snorting, squawking, squealing, yapping,
Huffling, snuffling, grunting, flapping,
Whinnying, trumpeting, bellowing, bleating,
Every kind of animal greeting.

OGDEN NASH

Squishy Words

(to be said when wet)

SQUIFF
SQUIDGE
SQUAMOUS
SQUINNY
SQUELCH
SQUASH
SQUEEGEE
SQUIRT
SQUAB

ALASTAIR REID

The Gobblegulp

The Gobblegulp is most uncouth
In his mouth is just one tooth
He gobbles food and gulps Ribena
Like a living vacuum cleaner.
He has a great big bulging belly
That wobbles when he walks like jelly,
But what I like about him least
Is that he is a noisy beast,
For when he eats an apple crumble,
His tummy starts to roll and rumble;
I often hear a noise and wonder,
'Was that a Gobblegulp — or thunder?'

COLIN WEST

He's Behind Yer

'HE'S BEHIND YER!'
chorused the children
but the warning came too late.

The monster leaped forward
and fastening its teeth into his neck,
tore off the head.

The body fell to the floor
'MORE' cried the children

    'MORE' 'MORE'

        'MORE'
           'M

ROGER MCGOUGH

Countdown

There are ten ghosts
in the pantry,
There are nine
upon the stairs,
There are eight ghosts
in the attic,
There are seven
on the chairs,
There are six
within the kitchen,
There are five
along the hall,
There are four
upon the ceiling,
There are three
upon the wall,
There are two ghosts

on the carpet,
Doing things
that ghosts will do,
There is one ghost
   right
      behind me
         Who is oh so quiet . . .

JACK PRELUTSKY

The Pod That Went POP

Five little peas in a pea-pod pressed,
One grew, two grew and so did all the rest.
They grew and grew and did not stop,
Until one day the pod went . . .

POP

ERROL CRISP

Song of the Pop-Bottlers

Pop bottles pop-bottles
　In pop shops;
The pop-bottles Pop bottles
　Poor Pop drops.

When Pop drops pop-bottles,
　Pop-bottles plop!
Pop-bottle-tops topple!
　Pop mops slop!

Stop! Pop'll drop bottle!
　Stop, Pop, stop!
When Pop bottles pop-bottles,
　Pop-bottles pop!

MORRIS BISHOP

Index of First Lines

Aeroplanes, aeroplanes all in a row	35
All day I hear the noise of waters	40
Billy is blowing his trumpet	15
Bishopsgate Without!	50
Boys shout	9
Chip-chop, chip-chop, Chipper, Chopper Joe	39
Come here to me, my merry, merry men	28
Crash and Clang!	17
Dad says	24
Down in yonder meadow where the green grass grows	41
Dumps beside the railway track	32
Every morning at six o'clock	19
Five little peas in a pea-pod pressed	60
He's behind yer	57
Humming-bird, humming-bird why don't you hum?	14
I can hear the trees whispering	19
If all the world's children	11
In the choir I'm a treble	18
In the greenwood stands a chapel	49
Jeremiah Obadiah, puff puff puff	30
Midnight's bell goes ting, ting, ting, ting, ting	48
My auntie plays the piccolo	16
My noisy brother's always noisy	22
O what is that sound which so thrills the ear	29
On the Ning Nang Nong	51
Once there was an elephant	52
Pop bottles pop-bottles	61
Puffer train, Puffer train	31
Rain is falling	47

Speak roughly to your little boy	25
Speedboats, bright blue, yellow and red	36
Squiff	55
The air was filled with a clamour appalling	54
The Gobblegulp is most uncouth	56
The panther roars on the mountain	53
The saddest noise, the sweetest noise	12
The wind has such a rainy sound	43
The wind was on the withered heath	44
There are ten ghosts	58
There's a cheeky snore, an' the squeaky snore	20
They line up together	34
Thud, bang, clash, roar	37
When I get angry I start	23
When the green woods laugh with the voice of joy	42
Whenever the moon and stars are set	46
Why should I always jump	26
You're only an ordinary animal	13

Acknowledgements

The Publishers and authors would like to thank the following for their kind permission to reproduce copyright material in this book:

Bogle L'Ouverture for 'Milk' and 'Humming-Bird' by Odette Thomas, from *Rain Falling, Sun Shining*; Cadbury Ltd for 'When I Am Angry' by Ian White, and 'Thunderstorm' by Danielle Brown, from *Cadbury's Fourth Book of Poetry* and 'Death of the Steelworks' by Caroline Lamb, from *Cadbury's Third Book of Poetry*; Jonathan Cape, the Executors of the James Joyce Estate, for 'All Day I Hear the Noise of the Waters' by James Joyce, from *Chamber Music*; Century Hutchinson for 'The Gobblegulp' by Colin West from *A Step in the Wrong Direction*; Robert Clarke, Literary Executor of Leonard Clarke for 'Speedboats' by Leonard Clarke, from *Collected Poems and Verse for Children*; Curtis Brown, London on behalf of the Estate of Ogden Nash © Ogden Nash for 'The Air Was Filled with a Clamour Appalling', from *The Animal Garden*; André Deutsch Ltd for 'Last Word' by Michael Rosen from *Don't Put Mustard in the Custard*; Faber and Faber Ltd for a four line extract from 'O What is that Sound' by W H Auden, from *Collected Poems by W H Auden*; Heinemann Young Books for 'Countdown' by Jack Prelutsky, from *It's Hallowe'en*; David Higham Associates Ltd for 'The Howling Pandemonium' by Eleanor Farjeon, from *Silver Sand and Snow* published by Michael Joseph, 'Bell-song' by Eleanor Farjeon from *The Children's Bells* published by Oxford University Press, 'The Mutinous Jack-in-the-Box' by John Cunliffe from *Standing on a Strawberry* published by André Deutsch; Marian A Lines for 'Railway Line' by Marian A Lines, from *Poems for Fun*; Spike Milligan Productions Ltd for 'On the Ning, Nang, Nong' by Spike Milligan from *Silly Verse for Kids*; The New Yorker for 'Song of the Pop-Bottlers' by Morris Bishop from *The Best of Bishop: Light Verse from the The New Yorker and Elsewhere* (Cornell). © 1950, 1978 Alison Kingsbury Bishop. Originally in *The New Yorker*; Peters, Fraser and Dunlop for 'He's Behind Yer' by Roger McGough from *Strictly Private*; Alastair Reed for 'Squishy Words' by Alastair Reed; Unwin Hyman for extract taken from *The Hobbit*, 'The Wind was on the Withered Heath', by J R R Tolkien.

Every effort has been made to trace copyright holders and the Publishers and authors apologise if any inadvertent omission has been made.